Strangers in Paradox

Carol Christenson

BALBOA.
PRESS

A DIVISION OF HAY HOUSE

Balboa Press books may be ordered through booksellers or by contacting:

Balboa Press
A Division of Hay House
1663 Liberty Drive
Bloomington, IN 47403
www.balboapress.com
1-(877) 407-4847

Because of the dynamic nature of the Internet, any web addresses or links contained in this book may have changed since publication and may no longer be valid. The views expressed in this work are solely those of the author and do not necessarily reflect the views of the publisher, and the publisher hereby disclaims any responsibility for them.

The author of this book does not dispense medical advice or prescribe the use of any technique as a form of treatment for physical, emotional, or medical problems without the advice of a physician, either directly or indirectly. The intent of the author is only to offer information of a general nature to help you in your quest for emotional and spiritual well-being. In the event you use any of the information in this book for yourself, which is your constitutional right, the author and the publisher assume no responsibility for your actions.

Any people depicted in stock imagery provided by Thinkstock are models, and such images are being used for illustrative purposes only.
Certain stock imagery © Thinkstock.

ISBN: 978-1-4525-3427-5 (sc)
ISBN: 978-1-4525-3428-2 (e)

Library of Congress Control Number: 2011905912

Printed in the United States of America

Balboa Press rev. date: 06/13/2011

Shhhhhh......

I want to know my God!
I cried, aloud, to the rising sun
I want...
I whispered, quietly, to the stars
I want...
I sobbed, desperately, into my pillow
Finally, a response:

Then, be quiet.

Ground Covers

Gazania and galaxies
grow toward each other
seeking to cover their respective ground
meeting, embracing, uniting
until all one sees are flowers...and stars

The Saturday Before Easter

Here I am
     caught between Good Friday and Easter Sunday
Removed from the cross
     and not yet risen from the dead
Like a caterpillar
      who, in its cocoon,
      am allowing all I've ever been
      to dissolve into all I will become
        … tomorrow

Religion

My poetry has been my religion
My link to Truth
My connection to God, whatever It is
I pour my life upon pages
    using words
        like a rosary
        like a mantra
        like a chant
    …repetition finally burning through ignorance
    until I see no reflection
Until what I write brings no tears
Because there is no space for them to form
And no time for them to appear

Rigidity

Time-space
is very pliable
before it molds itself into mass
with a face
   ...and a name

Reflections

Where in the world is Everywhere?
Is it in this world and beyond?
When in the world was it born?
Before the beginning dawned?
Why in the world did it come?
To give to world time-space?
Who in the world called it forth?
Ah...whomever wants to see Its face!

Alchemy

Now

...is a moment without boundaries

Space

...without time

God

...without a mirror

Yet

...to get here, one must traverse

    limitations

    clocks

    and reflections

Life

...is the path from nowhere to nowhere

    covering somewhere in its trek

Work In Progress

I am the inventor
of me

Each day I add
to my-ness
reforming it as I deem appropriate

I will never complete me

Done is a contradiction to forever

A Linear Circle

The shortest distance between two points
is not always a straight line

Sometime, it is no line at all

Ghost

There is more to leaving
    than leaving
If one leaves behind what should have been
    either taken or destroyed
    one must return
        or be haunted by the ghost of oversight

Silent Tears and Quiet Storms

My tears have gathered silently
Even I did not notice the clouds collecting in my life...
    birds still sang
    the sun still rose
    flowers, fragrant, still nodded to me as I passed
Life was beautiful
    but for the quiet storm forming in my heart

Some stores defy radar
They just appear...
You look out the window and all is black...
    the smell of rain permeating your life
    until, finally, you cry
    until there is not enough moisture left even for that rainbow
        you always believed in...
That, too, is gone

Then, clear and clean
    all Cinderellas and Princes Charming drowned
    all trust washed away
    all beliefs anchored to an old boat last seen sinking

Then, are you born!

A Master

I went into the wilderness of my self
to discover its secrets

How can I return and pretend
I did not find them?

How can I relate to those who think the wilderness is only for the brave
when, in fact, it is fear that prompts the journey?

How can I say that I searched for the Unknown
because I was afraid of the Known?

Need I say anything at all?

Perhaps I'll just be quiet

RSVP

Sometimes when I am alone
I am small and afraid
Surrounded by a fog that would
enfold me if I exhaled

I forget that it is but The Unknown
gently offering an invitation…

Sometimes when I am alone
I am taller than my fear
Surrounded by a light born from gray
that found its way to my heart

…because I said 'yes.'

Past Angles

When more and more obstacles block the door
cluttering my path with debris
I no longer worry, cause now I know
 it's my past that's in front of me

Light bounces off in angles
and what appears ahead
is really only what's behind
reflecting in front of me, instead

What is the thing you may, now, ask
that deflects the line of light?
Limitation within our brain
prevents us from taking flight

Between what we use and what we don't
is a ceiling of all known things
And those who think that it's the top
will never be able to grow their wings

Cause wings, of course, are known to most
as something for only birds
And, they'll never penetrate that roof
nor hear those unknown words

The only way I've found to fly
is to know that I can do it
It's knowledge that pokes a hole in tops
to allow its bottoms through it

Understanding, then, is that which takes
you over what's blocking you
and, once on the other side of it,
your wings appear...'cause you expect them to!

Missing Person

My passion dares me to learn who I am
and then to paint it, or write it, or sing it
thereby sharing with others my discovery
...not in deeds demanded by a society
            whose dictionary is obsolete
...but in colors I can only feel
...in words that mirror my soul
...in music that lifts me from the mundane

For I am what I create
And it's here
...hidden behind the letters of my life
...nestled in the tapestry of my heart
...secluded in the rhythm of my being
            where you will find me

Does Math Have Rhythm?

In my very humble opinion
the universe talks to us
In either math or rhythm
it cuts through all the fuss

It depends on if we're left brain
or if we come from right
How we pick up subtleties
hidden in the light

We may sing its praises with poems
or, in math, seek its mysteries
I wonder, sometimes, if perhaps
they both are the very same keys

To find the answer to who is God
is there reason in poetry?
Are they, in fact, both the same,
somewhere – in Eternity?

The Argument

Purple marks upon my heart
like bruises
only worse…
Stains
they are
left over from words
spilled by accident

Firewater

He, who expects the most
Me, who can only take so much

He, needing challenges
Me, needing peace from them

Why do opposites attract?
They say to make a whole

But we are blatant contrasts
Fire and water

Steam too much for me
…too little for him

The Leap of Faith

...took me from where I was
to where I am
The scenery is the same
...the main character is not

Question

A merry go round is like life:

    it has lots of ups and downs

    within an enclosed circle

To remove yourself from your wooden horse

    is to forsake the chance

    for a brass ring

But would it

    if you got it

    provide a gate to your coral?

And That Is Enough

To write about how life is
        becomes a blatant assumption
        that I understand it
If I understood it
        I would not be in such awe
        of its alleged mysteries
Yet, to wonder at its paths
        is more compelling to me than to simply choose the one
        that has been taken many times before
There is a place between
        deciding not to choose the well-traveled path
        and deciding which one to choose instead
                in which
                to make the necessary change
                one must understand Paths

In such uncharted territories
        there are no rules, no classes, no books
        to tell you "how"

There is only you to tell you why
...and that is enough

Butterfly Boredom

What does a butterfly do
      when it tires of even the flower's sweet essence?
It practices breaking sound barriers
      and time warps
It discovers there is more to being a butterfly
      than flying out of a cocoon

Breath of Life

I am melting
    somehow
What seemed real to me
    is now becoming liquid
    and unrecognizable in this new state
With no black lines to separate
    the good from the bad
    the right from the wrong
I am suspended
    somehow
    ...and I breathe different air

Cycles

Life oozes from us in increments of passion
     and metabolizes into emotion
     and coagulates into feelings
     and solidifies into form
          so we can see it
          touch it
          taste it
          smell it
          hear it
          and, finally, forget it
letting it fall from "real"
and crash silently
before breaking into bits of stillness
     magnetized by thought
     and reformed into passion

Old Souls

Some people touch my soul with intimate familiarity
  and sing it songs of tomorrow
Some people seek re-negotiation
  of contracts made beyond time
   showing me places where my signature is still legible
Some people strive to hold my glance
   long enough for me to remember
   something we are supposed to do together
    yet I answer their gaze with a question mark

Some people are persistent, though
   and insist on walking through the ghost town of my mind
   lighting candles along the way
Some people have a purpose of which I am a part
   and, refusing to go solo,
   they dance to my beat until I feel the rhythm
   and can remember the steps
    Bless them, those people!

Clear

Clear enough to be forever
     is my goal
Standing on a river bank
     and seeing, on the other side, a flower
     is not the same as inhaling its scent

The Visitor

I am different today than I was yesterday
for in the 'no time' between
> I perceived emotions that allowed 'time' to knock upon my door
> and demand to spend the night

What made me smile yesterday
may cause my tears today
> for the presence of my guest
> has changed me somehow

The cloak it wears hides even its face
and I long to tear it away
> to peer into its mysteries
> to learn its lessons

So tomorrow can visit me
unencumbered by my past
> and sit, welcome,
> at my table

Possible

Only when
      "destiny" and "now"
            are synonymous
                  will you stop trekking toward impossible

Only then
      will it reform in your lap
            content in its stillness
                  to make a nest and lay its eggs

Litter

The road to heaven is littered
    with the bodies of those
        who, not realizing it is dimensional,
           got trapped
                by the speed of light

The Art of Be-ing

Be-ing is an art
        one for which we all have unique talent

Each moment we create images of unparalleled greatness
        contributing, ultimately, to the
                Masterpiece of the Whole

We dab, erase, smudge, touch up, discard, re-create
        until we get a glimpse of The Big Picture

And, in awe, we are mesmerized by The Artist

It is here we lay down our brushes

Costumes

To soar...to fly above mediocrity
    yet never call it names
        is where my itinerary's headed
            cause I've played all its games

I've been both cowboy and Indian
I've worn costumes of the witch
I've been Cinderella several times
I've even been the bitch

I've loved them all...the parts I've played
    and learned an important rule:
        you can't enjoy the wise man
            until you've been the fool

Huh?

The universe
    is made
        of blobs of stuff
            held in place by each other

Dreams

Dreams heat life force
    causing stillness to move
        and movement to explode
            and explosions to simmer
                into wiser stillness

Dreams ignite will
    causing the birth of ideas
        and their creation into manifestation
        and their experience
            into the stuff that ignites bigger dreams

Going Within

Ignorance is an invisible fence
        keeping its captives caged within its walls
                while offering them information on freedom

Beings, there, are taught how evolved they are
        and, indeed, with no other information,
                it would seem so

Yet, they are confined by that which
        since they cannot see, touch, taste, smell or hear
                think is not there

But it is there
        and very real to those seeking freedom
                from something they can only feel

How does one climb an unseen fence?
        Within, of course
                where no one can see you do it

Light Happens

Light happens with no plug
     until we try to tame it

We break it into parts
     to control it

In pluses and minuses we manipulate it into
     co-operation and submission

Our lamp is lit
     even when, outside, the moon is shining

Co-Dependency

The flower
    too busy looking for the bee to bloom
        attracted it not

And then
    blamed her wayward counterpart
        for her extinction

The Enchantress

It is the moon that leads me
through the darkness of my dream
lighting pathways I only dare to imagine
while the sun
blatantly
defies the doorway to my cave

Light is an illusion

Its only purpose is to
allow the shadows
of what is real
to be illuminated

Definitions

A duality is like the North and South poles

...opposite ends of the same thing

...you know they merge...somewhere

A polarity is like adding East and West

...at right angles to the duality

...you know they merge...somewhere

A god is knowing they merge at the same place

A master is knowing the name of that place

An initiate is being able to get to that place

A Christ is being able to stay at that place

Invisible Circle

How I jumped
from the threshold of Now
into its center
is not nearly as important
as getting here

Once here
the how dissolves into the mist
that keeps Now hidden
from those
who do not believe
 in its existence

On Being Centered

Sometimes I move too fast
and
though I hurry
I cannot keep up with my self...
I look
but cannot see
where I went...
and
having left no trail
I often stumble...

Other times I am as fast
as I am...
Wherever I go
I follow
...easily!
Like a dance
...choreographed by God

Starry Starry Night

Night paints portraits
in silver and black
...like giant butterfly wings
spread across the sky
...color hidden by the moon

My Past

Dis-mantled...

Packed away
in memories unremembered

Resting in a peace
allowed only by its turmoil

Shadows now...

A vague fog
        in which lessons
                embalmed for preservation
                        lie in unrecognized pieces
                                somewhere
                                        behind me

Zero Point

A point, stirring

    becoming a vortex

        spewing energy

            in opposite directions…

Caught

    by self- inflicted boundaries

        and returning to its womb…

            dynamic now…Alive!

Holograms

We innertwine and we extertwine
     forming bonds, ropes and knots
From within to without and back again
     always interfering with each other's path

Eight

Only one way to lasso freedom:

    ...with its opposite

Want to keep something from evolving?

    ...tie it to its other direction

Emerging

My corners containing habits leak…

My past drips out behind me…

Drops of memories
      big and small
           puddle and
                cause a reflection
                    I cannot see

When all is gone
      drowned
           from who I was
              who, I wonder,
                will I be?

The Pain Cycle

Rage
from freedoms repressed
from singing suppressed
forced to anchor
ferment within us
until we are silenced by the "black box"
...and can no longer hear the words to our song

Instead
we sing with a genetic choir
songs of lifeless safety
until
the Truth we harbor inside
finally ceases to be restless
...and we die

Then does It emerge from its prison
...loudly proclaiming Itself!
Then do we remember our purpose
...and prepare, again, to carry it out!
Then are we reborn
...carrying our torch through the birth canal
...arriving full of spirit
into a body dependent upon outside forces
where
survival demands negotiation
...and our song, again, becomes a whisper

The Map

The road to heaven is paved in cloud colored graffiti
where fellow travelers
now content with time
have left their poetry
obscured in dawns and twilights:
        …look closely
                …read between the lines

Neglect

It's not that I did you wrong

It's that I neglected doing you right

I left

     to pursue my dreams within the hierarchy of my Self

         unencumbered by a body believing only in five senses

            and then returned

...to undo what I did by not doing

...to do what I now know how

Overtime

All the things I've never done
All the dreams unfilled as yet
All the songs I've never sung
All the goals still unmet

I pack into a bag, brand new
      and send back to their beginning
            for rearranging, for re-emerging
                  into the energy for another inning

Responsibility

I know the words to a bird's song
and hear in Coyote's cry the spirit of my poems

The breeze teases me with invisibility
but I know, too, her name

In the silent unfurling of a flower
I see the birth of a universe
and in a leaf the tapestry of a mountain

It is I who provide Nature her mirror

But for me she could not see her reflection
nor hear her echo

The tree nods confirmation
and I whisper "thank you"

It nods again
and I hear my laughter returned from yonder canyon

Peace: For Heaven's Sake

I spill over my top
I leak down my sides
  marveling how well
  all of me glides
I ooze as one stream
when soon I hit floor
  then inch across it
  and head for the door
Where ever so gently
between it and sill
  I squeeze myself into
  a place new and still
As I interact here
I leave in my wake
  a pattern of change
  for Heaven's Sake
I upon it make
a new hologram
  one where the lion
  lies down with the lamb

Gravity

What stays behind as I accelerate?
What is left when I boldly march into the wilderness of my mind?
What remains when I wonder what grows there
      and stare openly at the thriving gardens?
What cannot accompany my joy at choosing today's path
      and following it until I tire and nap by the river?
What refuses to keep up?
What ball am I chained to?
I do not recognize the face in my mirror
its face lined with undigested wisdom

Creation-Evolution

Glittering lights
illuminated by darkness
form a path
upon which I walk
choosing each step
as I make it
leaving in my wake
glittering lights
changed

On Time Control

Day: Then

Red mouth
open wide
swallowing
my itinerary
in gulps
easily digested
by such power

Day: Now

Sunrise
…an invitation!
Light
to be dressed
in my designer colors
and signed
with my name

Meditation

Like when an animal
stops and blends
I, too, am part of a background
…my stillness
recognized only by
those who dwell here

The Call

When you hear It

Answer!
...though Its voice gets lost in the crowd

Listen!
...until reality subsides in deference to determination
    and its sweet sound
        slides over the mountains
        with the dawn
           ...teasing you loudly with its color

Veils

Layers
no matter how sheer
if there are enough of them
appear solid

Mirrors

The only way to know who you are
is to be who you aren't
...till you squirm in your costume
...till you sweat in your mask
you will not know
there is more to life
than Halloween

Request

I don't have to see cause I know
but, at times, a peek would be nice
I don't have to hear as I grow
except, in doubt, when a sound would suffice

Just once when the sky is all black
and the storm looks camped for a while
It'd be nice if I'd develop the knack
of perceiving behind to its smile!

On Holograms

The gateway to forever is within
        then projected out
                in order to go through it

On Re-union

To still the tick
　　To quell the tock
　　　　To be the hum
　　　　　　And then the clock

Womb

When I turn in
completing my self
I am an egg
...concave and convex
...converging
...containing in each other
a yolk

The Magician

...so innocent in youth
weaving itself slowly among thoughts
young and naïve
enough to think Time is a playmate

...so adamant in age
now stitching faster and faster
thoughts tangled among its frequent threads
slowing the graying heads of playmates

...so deceptive in Truth
its patterns appearing real
to eyes that believe
only what they see

How To Heal World

1. Stop trying

2. Heal self instead

3. Resulting joy at accomplishment will automatically heal world

The Truth

Better to walk proudly
　　holding your bud secure
　　　　than to proclaim loudly your beauty
　　　　　　scattering your petals as proof

You

You
nourish me
…a young bud
too long in a dry desert
…petals contemplating suicide

You renew me
…adding rich soil to my base
…demanding I wriggle my toes

You provide water from an undiscovered spring
and hold the jug while I drink

I feel the surge of power

More, I feel the vibration of hope
welling up my stem
reaching my head
reflecting to my roots its completed course

My petals stretch
delighted in the warmth of noon
and wonder if, today, a car will pass
carrying a child able to notice a flower so beautiful
…and wonder why

Whale Song

In the ocean of air
throbs a current
heard by Cetaceans
who crawled from the sea
millennia ago? yesterday?
and now dwell in ancient skyscrapers
but hear, still, the song of the whale

Pervading the home of the eagle
vibrates a light
unseen by those
who walk crowded streets with eyes too glazed
to see the night skies and its entourage of stars

Permeating the space of our lives
there is a beat
felt by souls old enough to recognize its rhythm
and young enough to remember the dance

The Perch

It is amazing how
when you think of others
complexions clear
and ears hear their story
not yours…

Eyes shine
and divine energy
permeates the space between you
when you think of others…

It is amazing how
when you lose yourself to something bigger
like a drop merges with a river
"giver" enters your vocabulary
and stays…

Ways of healing the world
unfurl from your heart
like flags declaring an itinerary
…one worthy, finally,
of a place on God's bulletin board…

A space seen by all residents of heaven…

Angels then find you
…and wind their way to your shoulder

The Covenant

Only dancing bears remain on my horizon
now cleared of serpents and dragons
of devils and ghosts
and hosts of haunting memories...
It was I who suppressed them
denied their existence
forced them into a tiny space
where they fizzled and fermented and found ways to remind me
of their discomfort...
Some sneaked out and hid in corners
waiting to jump out from dark closets at night...
Some sang loud songs off key
until all I could hear was their plea for escape...
Until I could no longer pretend "fine"
while carrying "past" like a pregnancy
and delivering "future"
branded with the mark of the beast...
So I invited them to supper
where they told me their story
in ugly gestures and foul words
in screams of terror
in whispers of cowardice...
They spit fire
and hurled accusations
sending sensations of horror up my spine...

They whined, they moaned

and groaned of my abandoning them in the abyss of avoidance

where, unable to speak their peace,

they became war - and declared themselves on me!

"I'm sorry"

I said and offered them bread

"I understand"

I promised and passed the wine

until flaring tempers died in their own ashes

...and a new Covenant was signed

Incarnations

How long must images be held captive by half mirrors
reflections granted at the discretion of the wall upon which it is
hanging?

How long must bodies be imprisoned by half truths
realities passed out by paradigms in need of repair?

How long must brains be held in check by guards
too old to read a new language?

So that bodies and realities and brains
can echo more than teachings of books unburned!

The Pond

I am a pond
my waters stilled
until even my surface holds perfectly
the image of the Oak growing over my bank

I am a pond
old now and wise
with eyes that see clearly the sky
yet remember my youth
when truth was fed in pebbles
thrown into my depths
by teachers of innocence

How I rippled when betrayed
by boulders whose purpose, to teach,
drowned in route to my floor
leaving wakes of anger and pity stored
in currents that frightened small children
and sent them running from my shores!

How I moaned when stoned by bullies
playing games I did not understand
until a cloud stranded overhead by a storm
called loudly my name

I am a pond
my waters calmed by Compassion
learned from a reflection beyond even the Oak
…one whose outline above me I could not see
until so still was I
that even the sky did not ripple

Perfect Balance

Breakers
crash over
those who approach timidly
the sea

They threaten to topple
off balance
those not firmly planted
in their own shores

Presence

You steal into my mind
like an anti-burglar
leaving ideas like diamonds
in your wake

For my sake
priceless potential
glittering like gold dust
is scattered upon dreams, slumbering soundlessly

Upon awakening
I find I've been robbed!
Ancient nonsense no longer lies snug
in the jewel case once locked against thieves

Mute

What if my wall of words fell
surrounding us in paragraphs, incomplete
in sentences, unfinished
reducing my philosophy to an uncomfortable silence
rendering my ideas unknown?

What if letters fell from their ancient perch
like free electrons
invading other words
turning what still made sense into non-sense?

What if my wall of words tumbled down in a cacophonous roar
forming a puzzle from what was a metaphor
and dust from what was, before, a mountain?

Would we survive if communication were stilled upon tongues
       rendered neutral
...no words left to push into piles of right and wrong
...our free choice, like nature, now dependent upon intuition and instinct?

On Change

What causes things to change
to rearrange themselves into
patterns prettier than before?

What causes castle walls to crumble
humbling the architect who dwells within
sending her back to the blackboard
with a piece of fresh chalk?

What causes a mountain to become sand
and then an island waiting to be reborn?

What causes stars to slip from their perch
and streak across Night like a silent trumpet call
before falling into hands already holding wet clay?

What force can unglue something done
make its colors run back into pools of paint with no itinerary
and then give them a new agenda
watching with wonder the kaleidoscope turn?

Choice

Pain happens
Suffering is optional
Monsters are innocent
...until we paint their faces with ugliness

Dimensions

I dream of wings
but not of a bird

I dream of flying
but not through the air

I dream of knowing other lands
but not of this Earth

Layers of time
harbor secrets I want to wear

Shadows

The storm gathers quietly outside your window
casting shadows on the rug

And you
thinking it is only a passing cloud
do not notice the building of a tornado

Be aware
of tears cried only into pillows

Just Wondering

If a cell contains all of me
and an acorn carries the whole tree…
If in an egg is a baby whole
then what, I wonder, is the role
of whomever has the key?

I mean, what does God do all day
if Life survives by the word 'obey'?
Does She just rest and watch the show?
What does She do when She's feeling low?
To whom does God go to pray?

On Super Conductivity

I can only help you by helping, first, me...
To give only one-half of my Self
is to confine whole-ness by opposites
rather than complete-ness by likes...

Alive or Living?

Life
is like a bicycle:
Until you pick it up
and ride it
…it just lays there

Inner Critic

Everything I say is OK
My inner critic no longer shudders at every word heard
until my ideas stall mid thought
and fall into an untimely death

Everything I say is no longer up for grabs
its itinerary no longer questioned
Who cares the path my words take?
Who has a right to still them until they die of natural causes
and are buried on the outskirts of town
lest they are seen and recognized for what they are?

Everything I say I say firmly
Whispers no longer live in my soul
and hide when the doorbell rings

Victory

There will come a time when you have naught but your dreams
...when reality seems to fade into dis-solutions that demands your guest room
There will come a time when beliefs fall
...exposing their crumbling clay to the last ray of summer
and the wind, waiting its turn with you,
will reduce the remains to dust

There will come a time when you must know what is real
so that what is not can shed its cloak with no remorse...
so that what is false can collapse at your feet
without enticing a whimper from your soul

There will come a time when you will be accountable only to your self
...when what grows from the ashes of defeat is up to you
...when only in isolation can "Victory" be planted
...its sturdy stalk making its way to your house of dreams
and there, knocking loudly

There will come a time
when you will wonder what happened to your life
when you will think it some evil game perpetuated by some devil
too ugly to name
...until you hear that knock
and you peer out from behind your glasses darkened by distrust
to the essence upon your threshold
...and you open the door

Fear of Drowning

I am not perfect
I will never be perfect
As I stand here
rigid in false knowledge
I allow my self to soften into imperfection
…to liquefy from solidarity
…to relax my lines
…to release my fear
…to remove my doubt
…to know I can swim

On 'Me'

The 'me' that stares back
with wonder
with awe
The 'me' I see
angry
fearful
The 'me' who one moment is green
and in the next purple…
who says 'yes' to life
and then hides under its covers…
The 'me' searching for a way back
reflecting 'lost' one day
and 'found' the next
is me!
All me!
All facets of the same diamond
whose base awaits Its child's tales
like the father who welcomed home his prodigal son

On Truth

What is true today will not be so tomorrow

The kaleidoscope will change and another color will dominate

So I look at life with eyes turned inward to see my interpretation of their reflection...

and I hear you with ears needing confirmation from my heart before I nod...

I smell the rose with questions now

and taste in the sweetness of nature also its bitterness

To feel the fabric clothing me in all of its textures is to love burlap and silk equally...

I no longer care to be naked

Freedom is relative

It matters not what covering one wears

It matters only how one feels while it is being worn

The Co-Creator

In visualization do we architect our dreams
moving parts in the silence of our minds
until they please us enough to soften furrowed brows
and attract the building blocks of design
with which to shape our desire into a form...
the explosion of opposites now energizing our creation into life
which can then be colored with laughter and tears

Designer Stuff

Those who fall
upon the Creative Hologram
leave footprints
in its web

Designer patterns
upon Patterns of Design
combine
into firefly fashion shows

No purchase necessary
Wonder optional
Mystery revealed

Power Outage

A full forty five minutes of pure silence
No hum
No buzz
The full moon smiled

The Bridge of Faith

The Bridge
if you've built it
is crossed

To construct it
you must
step into the air

When it is complete
you are
on the other side

Roadblock

A boulder on my path
met me face to face
Too big to cross, too large to climb
it really slowed my pace

I looked around, I asked for help
to get beyond this thing
Lo and behold an answer came
and what a surprise it did bring!

"Tis not real – this block you see
Tis only in your mind
Something you <u>believe</u> has formed
a shadow – and you will find

that once this inner obstacle
now blocking where you're going
is reduced to rubble by <u>new</u> beliefs
its shadow will stop growing!"

Life

First you smell the flowers
Then you don't
They you do
The age at which you arrive at number three
is directly proportional to your
length of stay here

First you see the moon
Then you don't
Then you do
The degree of exhilaration felt at number three
is directly proportional to your
current state of health

Breathe deeply. Look deeply.
Beyond the scent and the sight is a trust
Connect with it
The degree to which you succeed
is directly proportional to your
ability to overcome anything

The Universal Path

Someone has to polish the stones
until they appear different
from the ground upon which they lay
and in their light create an
invitation to those able to reserve one

Someone has to provide handrails
for the parts that are steep
and bridges for the gaps that are wide

Someone has to trek ahead
to warm the soup
and turn the porch light on

Someone has to be there
to whisper "Welcome"
when weary, yet exuberant, travelers
find the door in the wall

Eternal-ness

As I bloom, I bud
As I reap, I sow
As I die, I live
As I learn, I grow
As I do, I dream
As I walk, I fly
As I go, I stay
And I know why

A Truth

Peace is a consciousness
that cannot be experienced
without the battle scars of war…
Even the 'peace that surpasseth all understanding'
has Armageddon's footprints in its belly

One Candle Power

So tiny yet so tenacious, my
candle at dawn…the one I turn on
as an indication for the sun to rise and
paint the skies with its rainbow brush

So somber yet so stimulating, my
morning light…the one by which I write my
soul's shadows upon white pages,
coloring me with fine, feathered strokes
until I am done

One candle power, one flame, one wavering
wonder attached to a wick that is
attached to eternity

One person, one human, one woman
wanting only to know that which
allows her to burn

Memories

There is such peace before the heart remembers...
The light of dawn has no wrong shades
nor notes sung out of tune...
All is fresh and young – too naïve to look at the sunset
still waving its red flags in a final attempt to
lure the lost traveler...
All is serene and as it should be before
yesterday awakens to cast its kindling into the fire
causing its flames to leap in frightened flickers
and threatening to burn more than the aged oak
stacked neatly upon the hearth

Peace

Warriors within
gather in a circle
hold hands
and pray for peace

Warriors within
look not behind them
nor count the casualties
of ignorance

Warriors within
focus instead
on one vision
seen by all

And they refuse to
paint their faces
nor beat their drums
nor don their shields

Until the color is wisdom
the rhythm is laughter
and the emblem is love

Waves

The I Am of who I Am washes the me of me
like ocean waves wash its own shore
to keep its individual grains of sand clean.

Unity

The last door to open is labeled 'Love'…
Its landscape taunts you with the perfume of beauty…
But when you stop to enjoy the fragrance of its flowers
a thorn appears to prick your heart and you leave a
trail of blood as fear causes your retreat…
Only the brave reach the threshold…
Only the courageous can see beyond Love's illusion
and are not harmed by the tricks it plays to seek only those
worthy of such an opening…
Only the wise understand…
The good and the bad are left outside Love's gate
believing, still, in roses and thorns

Caught in Time

Like a ball on a chain
I am caught in some concept...
Able only to swing through it
I grasp at its emptiness with
desperate fists...seeking a handful of
what it is that supports my trip.
But my palm, now open to expectancy,
contains only potential clay from which
I must build a destination...

Advice

It takes time to knock upon No Time's
door and be allowed into its silent domain…
But once there you don't care about clocks
ticking in incessant tocks nor how locks upon
pendulum swings brings relief from linear travel…
It takes time to hang suspended in a void
surrounded by currents just waiting to push and pull
naïve dreams into shreds…
But Stillness has collected you in its huge hand and
requested the honor of your Presence…
So don't exhale, now, nor wonder about those things
that go bump in the night when you are alone and frightened

The Debut

I am unraveling somehow...
A part of me got caught somewhere...
Probably snagged on a piece of faulty information...
I am being pulled from together by its understanding
and I see what my covering had kept hidden

I am frayed at my edges...
Loose threads dangle from my seams
threatening exposure

I am coming from together...
I am coming apart...
And whatever has been hiding in between
        is about to emerge

Walking Dead

Eyes glazed from watching screens instead of moons…
Songs silenced from singing tunes outside of Nature's range…
Ears buried by sounds other than birds at dawn…
The sun announces Day the way a pregnancy announces birth…
Yet the window shades are still down…
Curtains drawn against the intrusion of possibility

Humble

Sometimes I get caught up in my own
grandeur and I chatter like a shallow wave
caught in the wind...
Only when I allow myself to sink deep into the sea
does my restlessness surrender to quiet humbulations

Re-pair Work

I am where I'm headed
I am already "there"
"Here" is its name
The place is quite rare
It's found in the middle
Or don't you care
To arrive in between
Such an awesome pair?
It's worth the trip
That much I'll share
What you find is yourself
What you fix is a tear

Is ...is

I am
the water within the wave
I ride with it
up and down
up and down
up and down
I laugh, I cry
I feel the pain and joy
of sorrow and bliss
But I am not up nor down
I am up and down
because water is water

Television

Information is fed with silver spoons
laced with bright lights and whirring noises
to disguise its effect...
And we – too smart to see beyond the TV screen
eat heartily, flipping through commercials
because they are stupid

Tornado

From no thing
to a wisp
to a fluff
to a light piece of itself
to rain and wind
to hail
to thunder and lighting
until sky meets ground on a mission
then fades
to gentle-ness
to fluff
to wisps
to no thing
Such is me…
And you…
Such is God
There is no such thing as opposites

Master Builder

Building mountains is more fun than building buildings
Climbing them is more challenging than being enclosed in them
Reaching the summit is a goal more worthy than reaching the penthouse
And sleeping under the stars more restful than under a mirrored ceiling

Immortality

The End
...is The Beginning
Something old dies
Something new is born
...sometimes in the same container

Awareness

The sky is dusty...
Clouds once light and white
or heavy and gray
are now just thick with indecision...
Air once moving on a breeze labeled "Spring"
or riding the back of an unbroken hurricane
seems content to stall over this blue-green planet like a gray question mark
seeking an answer, still
but no longer demanding one

What will happen if we don't see curiosity waning like a fading moon?
Or the stars becoming hazy as they near the exit?
Or the sun, looking like a foreign dictator in its unfamiliar colors?
Or the trees closing early – feeling Winter's empty marquis long before
      the glass is broken by harsh winds and the letters blown away?
Or the flowers never reaching maturity – dying, instead, like youths sent
      to war with nothing but "Innocent" stamped on their forehead?

What will happen to Life if we can't see It wondering what will happen
      to us if we don't see it leave?

Timeless

Time has flexible bars
      once outside
            of its inflexible cage

Duality

Everything has a dark side...

A place where it is connected to the unseen world...

Roots that feed what is seen, keeping it alive...

What we call Death is simply a root...

The other side...

Like Winter to Spring...

A time to go within...

To retract, to rest...

Death provides a way to remember our heritage...

To re-unite with that which allows us to be born...

Like Spring from Winter...

New now, refreshed from its nap

The Masks

Sometimes
when you look at me
I don't see your face...
I see masks and am consumed by their meaning
their memories hidden in the crevices of paper mache
their messages written in brightly colored paint:

>the warrior
>
>the healer
>
>the mystic
>
>the teacher

all rolls
...personalities played on other stages
daring me to undress them
...but you turn too soon
and all I see
is the back of your head
...leaving

Auto-Immune Disorder

A body attacking itself?

It is as preposterous as humanity declaring war on itself!

What kind of God could create a clock where Noon's bells violate
        Midnight's chimes?

Trinity

Paradox happens when opposites cross
When two things 'are' but shouldn't be
It happens because One is Two
No, really, One is Three!

From the place of intersection
'Whole's' mystery oozes in
Dawn's a paradox - so's dusk
Are they really kin?

Yet those accustomed to only half
See dawn as just day's hue
And dusk as the bringer of the night
And a child as pink OR blue

New Word Order

I think it is time
for new words to be born
Most of the old ones
are tattered and torn
They've been over-used
over-worked and they're tired
Let's give them a rest
before they get fired
Let's mold some new meanings
which make a new sound
So that what's being learned
can get off the ground
It's hard to take flight
when anchored to past
We need some new props
and new members of cast
Or, perhaps all we need
is just to be still
Perhaps being quiet
can fill better the bill
It's hard to describe
what's now taking place
Maybe NO words at all
would hasten our pace

Life

Hands hold....

Fingers fold to contain
...or to crush
that which is being held...

Until fingers open to free
that which has survived
...or to let fall
that which has not...

Evolution

To unfold too quickly
is like watching the sun rise
while thinking about breakfast
...you miss the subtle change of color

Patterns

Moments are Time's children...

In tiny increments they emerge from the Womb of Forever

in search of sustaining a dream...

Born whole, they separate at birth in order to lasso a wild desire

and hold it together, molding it with cosmic fingers until it is formed,

coloring it with bright possibilities until it is lived,

and then allowing it to fall from grace when it is forgotten...

Until only a residue remains – the dust of desire:

...moments, again free

Broken Connection

Brain-Heart
Soul-Spirit
Mind-Body
All the same....
Intelligence-Feeling
Philosophy-Experience
Time-Space...
Until we emotionalize
our understanding
there is a gap the
size of our ignorance...

Sacred Circle

To leave and return to
To go and to come from
Around and around
Again and again….
To join the center
To be still
While Life surrounds you…
Leaving – returning
Going – coming
Around and around
Again and again…

The Gap

Time
pressures me into a beam...
Makes me focus...
...zero in
to get things done...
while
it stresses me into a frazzle...
Makes me hurry
...spreads me out
to get things done...
As
it ticks its merry way
toward Heaven

The Cloud

My duty as a cloud is to create rain

...not to worry about which flowers will get watered when it falls

Chaos?

Am I going or coming?
I wonder
as I always seem to reach a wall tall enough to
stop my forward thrust – or is it backward?
It's hard to tell these days, the direction…
Only the blocking of it is real…
It's the bumping into it that reminds me I'm moving,
the stopping that tells me I've been going…
Bur where?
I wonder
as I panic and stare at the blackness in front of me –
or is it behind?
I don't know anymore, the direction…
Only that it is interrupted often

Narrow Gate

Without opposites to hold them
things would fly away...
Gravity isn't a thing, you know
It's a result of extremes – OK?

Life exists in the middle...
between the sides of "All"
Tis there where movement moves
from side to side of wall

But

In between the sides is "One"
From side to side is "Two"
So is it any wonder that we
haven't got a clue?

But

God is really "Three"
and it's we who choose the way...
To return we either walk the line
or choose to ricochet

Walking on Water

Regaining the rhythm is what it's about...
Re-stirring the stardust - enabling its emergence
      to settle into patterns easily walked upon...
Re-configuring the constellations is what it's about...
Re-birthing a path across the vast blackness that
      is their womb...
Re-lighting the light is what it's about...
Re-writing the map so that it now includes
      directions to Heaven...

The Hug

What if the sun took a sabbatical?

What if it deserted the troops in the trenches and went off to Orion

to learn how hydrogen becomes helium?

What if, on the day war was scheduled to begin, dark did not dim

and dawn did not arrive with its red flags waving readiness?

What if soldiers, carrying weapons loaded with hatred, squinted

their eyes in tries to find the uniforms colored differently from

their own and only a background of black surprise returned from

such perplexity?

What if the other side got restless as the skies refused to grant the

go-ahead?

What if both moved toward the center – arms outstretched like

white sticks – until encountering skin, warm like their own,

they could fill a moment with wonder rather than wounds?

A Rainbow

We do it within these clay bodies of ours. The ones that
dry and crack in the light, calling night in with damp towels...
She surrounds us with peace and allows the grains of sand
caught by day to become pearls of wisdom before healing our
sores with moondust...

When the sun comes up, we can chose either to remember
the mouth of the river, or to return again to the sea – too
brittle for anything less than complete immersion...
We do it within this atmosphere that hides many colors
in its invisible folds – each one housing golds like seeds of
various Truths...

We do it here. We do it now. Nothing changes....except us.

On Love

Love softens…
It rounds sharp edges,
smoothes corners, creates circles where
once were angles, hard

Love tempers…
It melts inflexibility, becomes pliable,
changing what was rigid into something
fluid and curious

Love allows…
It forgives ignorance, grows tolerant,
causing what was formed in fear to fall
away, return to dust

Fly Fishing

The ground was ugly...
Gray stones that all looked the same...
Weeds that poked confidently
from cement chipped by time's tenacity...

I lay on my back a lot, back then...searching
heaven for shooting stars instead of God and
anticipating the full moon more than the second
coming of Christ...

Reality was dirty. Anger was planted in it like
a mine field and I learned to walk very carefully
even to that place that allowed, without questioning
my motives, my desire to flee from whatever was
currently suffocating. And, there, I would be content
to watch clouds change shapes and wonder if it were
true what they said about rainbows...

I was a dreamer..."just like your Father!" admonished
my Mother more than once and, each time, I felt a
red hot pang of guilt try in vain to be recorded...

But butterflies were prettier than caterpillars and
birds were free to fly home for the holidays...

And then, just when my last desire was tied to the line
and cast into complete silence with held breath, I exhaled
too soon or something. Maybe a sneaky shadow
caught me off guard, causing me to shift my focus.
Because I returned…empty handed and barefoot,
but able to see that gray had many different shades and
that there is tapestry even in cracked cement.

Please

Everything I want is right here – right now…
Every place I've headed, seemingly in vain, is hiding
in the shadows of where I am…
Every person I've wanted to hug is waiting in some
corner of my life for my embrace…
Every one I've longed to speak with is dancing around
my head in disbelief that I've not yet heard their voice…
I am sitting in the middle of Forever! Always!
Its boundaries are self-made by my thoughts and if a box
is formed that keeps me caged within the limits of humanity,
I am my own guard for I, alone, have the key to my cell…
All around me is Life – ebbing and flowing in distinct
patterns named Infinity and I am a current in them all…
I can feel this like the beat of my heart trying hard to capture
this moment for its posterity – and mine – and all I can do
to keep from exploding is close my eyes and whisper…

Middle

Each time you pull tighter, the knot gets smaller.

Each time you let go, the rope gets larger...until
the knot disappears and the rope becomes too big
to see.

Both become All

Is God Dead?

In the beginning there were two mirrors. One on the
ceiling and one on the floor. They played vertical games
of Who's Who until Ignorance entered their domain and
obscured the ceiling with her veils of deceit. The floor mirror
had no alternative, in order to preserve the reflective tradition,
but to crack into two: one for me, one for you

And we spend our lives searching each other's face for signs
of God – all the time wondering where It went

The Second Coming

We dive into Life like freedom fighters…our
wings glistening with iridescent truths. We do our acrobatic
dances that defy even Heaven, dipping here – stalling there,
flashing our goals with polished precision

We then join teams, form formations…no longer acting out
harsh itineraries in solo steps. Instead, we soar through the skies with an
assurance born of numbers – too busy watching the choreography to
notice the tarnish beginning to crust outside the cockpit

Until Winter forces us to land - often with rusted gears - and climb
painfully out of our enclosed world, its windshield now cracked

Only then can we notice, with eyes newly opened, how good feels
the solid ground…how green is the grass

Corners

At a corner, one must make a choice…
And going in the same direction is no longer one of them…
For some reason, your options have changed and corners
are Life's way of letting you know…
At a corner, all decisions are narrowed down to a single
point – their culminated possessions extending in either direction…
At a corner, it is necessary to pick one – only one – narrowing
your life line in half and following it on only one leg…
But, at a corner is a secret: all the stuff you no longer want
goes one way and all the other stuff goes the other.

Surrender

Upon leaving the ground, one forfeits the right to smell
the flowers growing there…
One sacrifices words and sounds that abound within
the details of a closely woven reality…
One relinquishes, too, the weeds still thriving and
the wounds still bleeding

To gain altitude automatically assures an adventure,
a view from a different dimension, an ability to see
more colors of the tapestry than your own

To soar is to invite The Unknown into your changing
purpose…to allow it to settle where it will,
sometimes stirring your new destiny with a muddy stick

But to arrive, one must let go of the controls…
release man made charts…toss out of the disappearing
window all maps heretofore pointing the way to Heaven

Fog

Meditation is my medication
It aligns me with my proper perspective
It reunites me with harmony
It restoreth things defective simply by reducing their visibility to zero

It re-pairs and re-joins my duality so that the competition between them ceases due to lack of space

Their mirror is reduced to one with two sides rather than two mirrors with a place in between for misunderstandings

Whole

Going solo requires only one thing:
You, no longer divided

Names

It's words that trip me, falling from my mouth unannounced
and causing a bump in my road that can catch my heel if I'm too
busy wondering where I am going to notice where I am

It's vocabulary that does an injustice to my itinerary, often
falling short of my planned destination and necessitating a stop
to survey any damage caused by an innocence, unaware

It's letters, put into packages, supposedly meaningful, that attempt
to convey my identity. Yet they leave in my wake only an outline
too solid to penetrate and my real name remains an echo longing,
still, to be heard

Only in silence can I tell you who I am…and hear, as well, you. But
 if the ears with which we listen are addicted to sounds twisted into
patterns, we will hear only the world's definition of our identity

Metal of Honor

Spiritual alchemy is the process of trusting
the fires to stop burning...turning to light instead
of to ash that which is being burned

You must wait beyond the time tested as tried
and true to do that which you came here to
accomplish

You must let Patience preside over Doubt's
assembly until all leave for lack of motivation
and you are left with an emptiness devoid, even,
of echoes

And, finally, you must be willing to test the
purity of the metal remaining in your crucible
...by wearing it

Doubt

When Now finds your heart and removes the
'No Vacancy' sign posted there in fear, don't look up
nor down. Don't look left nor right to see if it is OK
to allow its entrance to your controls

Look only within for the light of your next step and
then without to see where it was placed

When Now awakens your soul with songs of humility,
listen only with ears turned inward for the next word, using
those pointing to the world only to hear horns honking to
warn of oncoming traffic

Then

Stay tuned to the middle, even while moving in
directions all around, to avoid the dangers of
doubt

Remain focused on that place from which movement is
born but which is always still because it trusts its own
reflection more than the mirror created by uncertainty

Cinderella Revisited

I remained in the closet, softly, allowing the darkness there
to muffle fear's cackle and cover its illusion long enough for me
to see through it

When finally ready to emerge, I did not open the door gently
nor tiptoe out quietly. No, I quite surprised myself by jumping
into the light, both feet jarring the fragile floor with loud
determination

Then, magic wand in hand, I abracodabraed my way to the
castle attracting princes charming enough but lacking in the qualities
necessary to appreciate the beauty of frogs

So I lived not very happily until Ever After visited me in the garden
and explained to me how midnights always become dawns...carving
pumpkins made of glass

Inside Out

Creation is the act of defenselessness becoming defensive…
Of naked becoming clothed, but knowing not what it is wearing
Evolution is the removal of the layers of innocence…item by item
is each examined and then discarded, leaving an echo of wisdom
in its place…
Until all that remains is nakedness, internally defensive now, due
to the experience of wearing itself

Lessons

Knots happen when objectivity no longer rules...
It is the observer who simply watches, guiding every move
from a perspective of wholeness...
Personality is the culprit...
When what simply IS becomes internalized as more than simply
wisdom, knots form...
When what is being experienced is felt not as just information but
as a personal assault or as personal praise, loops lock karma into
their folds - for what is taken in must be given out...
It is the necessity for give and take that keeps us coming and going...
We must learn to be as silk and allow lessons to simply slide from us,
depositing truth in our hems as they leave

Caught in My Cocoon

One leg is lagging behind ...
still looking for glimmers of goo that was you, yesterday
or me, wandering through the ashes in search of songs still
hummed when least expected...catchy little numbers whose
emotions are still experimenting with hormones too hot for safe
sex, causing the unwed pregnancy rate between the memories
 to rise in proportion to the pain unleashed

While the rest of me wants to run from this place...to take off from
the ground, suddenly, feeling the wind in my face like a fan of
freedom, this foot still trips among the cracks, catching itself
on some raised portion of yesterday – its darkness like a shadow
across my runway

Warning

Doubt bombards the borders and creeps into
cracks left unattended by Love

It rains on parades of Knowingness
if left too long outside the door to your heart

It is a master at treachery and a Ph.D of
deception, using smiles and pretty words to
lure you into its cave only to seduce you
with kindness

Then it releases you…back into the world
where you walk, but no not where

Boundaries

Animals establish them with pee

People establish them with war

Masters establish them not

The Best Defense

Become defenseless to defend against that which
would hold you hostage to its world…for it empowers
its boundaries with only the fear of its prisoners

Drop your weapons if you would seek release…and
discover that such an act dis-covers that which hides
escape

But let not the surprise of this effortless effort surprise
you for "Doubt" hides in its folds and nothing closes this
Self-made opening faster than a self-made door

Evolution

First there was a candle with a tiny, little wick
anchored in "Forever" till the wind caused it to flick
Then came the god "Electric" to keep us safe and warm
when the wind that put the candle out became a frightening storm
Finally, superconductivity rode in on steed of white
to assure continued light all through the three-day night

The Quickening

Artificial lights blink faster
Artificial sounds come louder
Artificial life moves more quickly these days...

Darting eyes tell all...

Thoughts interrupted by themselves fall, like
aborted fetuses, into the vast wasteland of
incompletion...

Connection, once severed, is repaired not by speed
but by will...

Faster, louder, brighter is like a Christmas tree
to which one adds more and more ornaments – all
the while losing the beauty of simplicity and the
magic of the season

Awakening

A Christ is one in whom the projection has
served its purpose and been withdrawn…

Such withdrawal releases the power sustaining it
to the source of its extension…

Such release reconnects the source of its extension
to the source of creation…

Such reconnection eliminates the darkness that
appeared to separate that which is inseparable…

Such elimination restores the light…

Such restoration ends the dream

Reunited

In reconnection is clarity returned

In reparation is knowledge restored

How long I traversed the darkness
matters not...for

In recognition is separation ignored

Fire and Light

Pluck a star from the sky if you dare
but be careful of your stance...
To reach with one arm only
may cause a fall – when you want a dance

To take some light from dark is fine
but better be whole when you do...
For stars can burn when caught with one hand
yet are comfortable when resting in two

Who Are You?

I dress family and friends in my favorite colors
demanding they obey my style and wear only the accessories
      chosen by me...
I love looking at them – lavishing them with well-earned praise
      as they speak clearly their lines and laugh right on cue...
But – who are you
      when the sun sleeps and only the stars outline your nakedness?

Definition

Born naught but my Self
naked of pretense…
Love, raw and wild, seeking but a definition
became defined…
A body
clothed in tools of survival
but harboring a fugitive…
A name that begins and ends
yet contains a middle which no one knows…
The "Self" that refuses to be adorned in perception
        nor perceived in concepts
but chooses – always – the freedom to be what Love is
regardless of the apparent rules enforced by the
        illusion of a definition

Sustenance

In fear
I gathered wood and water
for later, when I would be cold and thirsty

I herded Beauty into the arena of my mind
in case I should find a time when Ugly visited
and stayed too long

But a wind blew my house away,
scattering the wood pile and spilling the water.
And the memories stored so lovingly forgot themselves.

I have only The Moment: Now, in its full emptiness.

Compassion

First I was the blossom
    taking from the limb

Then I was the limb
    taking from the trunk

Then I was the trunk
    taking from the root

At last: I am the root
    giving to the tree

The Altar

We learn fear, then think it real
enough to wrap our innocence in,
covering completely, what breathed us
into being

We design our 'self' to fit our needs
molding desires into dreams that have a
price tag no one can afford, yet many attempt
to purchase

And we, too naïve to understand the value
of our soul, bargain and barter until bitterness
becomes exhaustion…we then unlock our secrets
and wonder what they are worth

It is there we find the table of exchange.
Sensing something too deep to be found, yet
wanting nothing more than to find it, we begin
to disrobe…laying that which held us hostage
upon The Altar

Thus dis-covering a miracle

The Choice

The hologram shifts so quickly these days
colors, once clear, are becoming haze...
The dance speeds up as the music plays
faster, now, its steps a maze...
All participants in expressions of daze
wrinkled and crumbled like crackles in glaze...
Yet, the moon still shines in cosmic rays
and does its magic in taunting phase...
Rather than he who only betrays
creation Itself and Its myriad ways...

Shift

When my mind is clogged, it knots my brain
and clarity becomes quite tangled
My body, which mirrors such confusion
gets nervous – and becomes all jangled

Then who I think I am's unclear
and it acts on such a thought
When what, instead, I need do
is be still…and become a dot

A vortex to – Forever!
where no thing's in the way
And, clearly, the one I know I am
is recognized above the fray

A moment, no more, is all it takes
for the return of clarity
So when I come back to where I was
I am no longer me!

The Fall

When Love fell and
shattered into tiny pieces,
each naked and unrecognizable,
masks were made to cover

Love's innocence and protect
Love's beauty. Named Fear,
named Anger; called Bitterness,
called Betrayal, they wove their

colors into patterns of such
intricacy one would not notice
the subtle-ness of each charge
nor feel anything but something

when paper mache life did not
match the sunrise. Life is a process
of putting the pieces back together,
one by one...painstakingly...clearing

each fragment only by the wearing
of it. Until enough shards, gathered
together, can then reflect Love's
coherency, it is necessary to adorn

oneself with each sharp point. Only
when the day dawns bloodless can
Love be known as The Creator....
even of Hell.

Underground Spring

Hidden below the hills and valleys yet
nurturing each with the same flow, I strive
for clarity by clearing myself of debris
still clinging from childbirth. Far from

the open wounds of the blood-stained
battlefields, I participate not in the war
but choose instead to heal the reason for its
existence, the laws that allow it to triumph

...breaking into pieces the coherency
built by intrepid souls. Away from the brave
who are willing to declare their truth, often
inciting battle with but the cry for peace, I

wander...sometimes dissolving into but a
drop...but never disappearing. I no longer
cry at the beauty being beaten into the gray
stones now being carried seaward, nor do I

laugh with the daffodils who defiantly declare
Spring regardless of the Winter recently endured
...though I tickle their toes with appreciation
as I pass. I see it all, now, and it is (all) good.

On Middles

I was old even when in a child's body
and I am young while lined and gray...
There is a Way within that is mine: my truth, my light
offered always, but taken only when the heart rests
between its hills and valleys

Middles keep highs and lows from coming apart
by encasing each with its opposite

One – or the other – is the cause of all sorrow. For both
are the same: connected to Forever and nursing at Her
breast, a child....hungry for Life

It is the middle I want to assuage....this neutral I need to
massage back into peace and hold it still long enough
for the Love to dry.

Living

Born again and yet again...
Renewed each moment...
Life...a drop of Forever
  caught by the hands of Time
    and molded into steps
      that choreograph my dance

Mirrors

I attract not only an "opposed" movement but
one who holds within it my secrets. I see in him
'not me!' – yet stay, turning him over and over,
looking closely until he becomes his version of
who I was and I find reflected in my new smile
his eyes.

Ears to Hear

The warnings howled upon the winds,
rattling windows and causing even brick
houses to fall down

Yet, in the distance, the loudspeakers
played mesmerizing music…its rhythm not
at all interfering with the hum of television
nor the buzz of computers

Denial

I was as surprised as any to find 'Ugly' blooming
in my garden marked 'Beauty Only.'

How could it disobey my desire for Perfection,
blatantly poking its head above ground for all to
see!

I withheld water and blocked the sun with a black
blanket. But it thrived.

Only when I picked its flowers for a bouquet
did it go away…leaving clean dirt in its wake.

Suffering

Ego dies in pitiful cries.
It leaves a wake of wailing torment
in which a god is born…emerging from
the noise in silent wonder, a crown of
thorns its echo.

Self-Worth

Self-made, from the fabric of clay…
Potential pottery, nothing more…
self, first, a baby born with only five senses
      crawling, walking, running, skipping and dancing
            thinking that, surely, nothing more is possible…

Then: rebirth!
Self, born with only the understanding of wings
      yet having to crawl, walk, run, skip and dance before
            finally flying to instigate their worth.

New Year's Eve

Tears
Crystal towers
Crumbling
Streaks obscure the view
    held by force
        yesterday

A thought
Only that
And today rains, torrential,
    blur the world I used
        to live in

The Illusion

I'm not a part of this world
I never was I see
I only thought I was
When I got trapped inside of me!

Bridgeless

There is a gap I must bridge
between my feelings and my words...
Intense love pours from my heart
fills my mind
finds solace in my soul
and waits
for a chance to explode
into meaning, passionate
into embraces, gentle
yet...
when I see you...
I cry

Midnight Awakening

Have I poured out enough of my past
to allow a New Year space to settle in,
comfortably?

No longer too crowded to unpack its
itinerary and stay until the wrinkles
hang out?

Have I left the walls bare enough
for new art to be hung – no longer competing
for a place to leave a personal message?

Have I left the light on
brightly enough, this time, so that you won't
pass me by – thinking me asleep?

Creation

It is an art...
Free-form thinking
allowed to solidify
into colors, vibrations, words

Into forms
that reflect a way to
portray thought

Rules are non-art...
Formed patterns allowed
to find only the familiar
mold and, there, to sleep soundly.

Co-Creator

It's my desire that causes energy to become both a
fairy god-mother and a wicked step-mother…
A witch rides in from both the East and the West
when we send our dreams into the Cosmos to do their
dance of magic…
It's my wants that send particles of energy careening
into each other like quantum suns, exploding to share
their 'each' with 'all' and allowing the new creation to
name itself…
It's my needs that dictate to Time how long this creature
need gestate and it is my feelings at its birth that will
determine the length of its stay

Moss

As Light evolves, more information is available.
First, within us, as miniature universes explode into
understanding. Then, reflected outward as we see
for the first time, though we have looked before, Life.

Clearly, now, runs the stream…every pebble polished
cleanly enough that denial no longer grows like a fungus,
hiding truth under the pretense of beauty.

All is visible and all is beautiful. Even the ugly, because
now we can see it. And the bruises made black by
suffocation may turn purple and, then, heal.

Choice

I was trying to write my own script, map my own journey,
sing my own song...one that bent the rules, though not out
of dis-respect, written by Heaven.

I was trying to make my own way, color my own dream,
write my own poem...one that deviated from the truth, though
not because I am a rebel, learned by those who came before.

I am but a seeker of Truth and though all known paths offered
me their flowers, I could pick but a few of each to prevent
being burdened by a bouquet too large to see, clearly, the
step I chose to take.

Above Rubies

Above the repercussions of my ignorance
I find my mind
wandering...not aimlessly searching for The Door
but within The Room – endless, timeless...
Already content, complete.
Already a part of Forever

Above the repercussions of my ignorance
I find my mind
wondering – not helplessly carrying The Question
like a burden – but within The Answer...
Already contained
Already a part of God

Above the repercussions of my ignorance
I find my mind
at peace...seeing war wandering aimlessly, disconnected
and wondering helplessly, hopeless...
somewhere below
somewhere non-existent

9-11

It crashed in on me too quickly
imploding before I learned to leave...
Fallout blocking stairways and stopping
elevators, mid floor...
Debris, never filed, flailing wild arms
and wondering where to settle – still hasn't...
Messes are made deliberately, like war.
It is peace that suffers, lying under the chaos
like a floor, polished clean.

Return to Co-Creation

Contained
>   but by forever
My Love
>   Is free to fly
Confined
>   but by eternity
My Life
>   I give to 'I'

Connected
>   but to my Self
My Light
>   is free to flow
Darkness
>   no more demands
That I
>   carry it in tow

Just Sit

Be a rock in a river
 anchored to its ancient bed...
When currents caress your head with
 playful fingers

Just sit.

Be a boulder in a stream
 firm in its eternal foundation...
When life splashes all around you
 threatening to toss you off balance

Just sit.

Be an island in the sea
 born before time...
Allow the surrounding waves to wash over you
 in cycles, necessary to growth, and

Just sit.

Be the sides that make the middle
 the ones untouched and, therefore,
 untangled by what flies by at speeds
 approaching sound and light, leaving a
 wake of cries in the dark...

Just sit.
Just sit.

Rebirth

Then…tears and laughter collided in my heart
like some conflict finally resolved…
Leaving me without a name…no mirror with which
to see my reflection…
Where opposites, yesterday, formed pools in which I swam,
today is empty…
Only a seed…a pod holding only potential…breathes
in gentle whispers…
Inhaling energy from some unseen force,
then exhaling, forming what is unafraid to live among the ruins…
An egg now…
A pregnancy, carried softly

Ebb Tide

Often
I well up with love
like an ocean that is too full
and can find no outlet…
My heart cries in joy
yet I know not where to sing
nor whose ears will recognize my song…
And then it is gone…
I recede…
My heart's wave ebbs in disappointment
that I, again, let the moment pass
without saying anything
to anyone

Cremation

Like the ashes of a loved one's body
so our past is simply a collection
of fired neurons stored in a memory
rather than an urn...
Both are rendered useless for the same reason:
the experiencer has departed

Mandelbrot...

God is
> the same pattern
>> enfolded upon Itself
>>> in infinite layers

We who
> unfold the levels
>> like peeling an onion
>>> discover the core

and laugh…

Sheer joy
> awaits those willing
>> to traverse the tears
>>> to get to the truth.

With Age Comes Wisdom

In my innocence
I gave my enemy
ammunition

Then I didn't
believe in
enemies nor ammunition

Now…
I don't believe in innocence

Reflections

I feel like a lake, satisfied with its youth…
Content, now, to simply reflect the sky rather
       than compete with it…
One who is lost in its own depths – so that even
       the storms that thrash across its mirror,
       shattering Heaven into pieces of light and dark,
       sounding trumpets like war cries – ruffle it not.
One who allows the deer to drink from its fountain
       without feeling threatened with depletion…
And the Oaks to see their lovely faces without envy…
And the fish to flash their iridescence with no desire to glitter…
One who simply understands the sun…who has found the source
       of reflection…so is content, finally, to cease searching
       for it.

Sabotage

Resentment strong…
Spirit weak…
I tried to destroy the vessel
…too ignorant, then, to know
it was carrying me

Sea calm…
Boat fixed…
I sail with flag unfurled
…too wise, now, to be lured
into unsafe harbors

Free Choice

I'd rather watch the sun rise than set...
Eyes, wise, from being the recipient of many dawns
      wonder, still, at its colors...
How it manages to dress its days in ways that announce
      to the world its moods...
Then, once awakened, allows Day to have its way...
To stay the theme breathed into it by desire for change,
      once born, demonstrating its own personality.
Like a babe, once weaned, can remain a reflection of its
      parent or become a being with its own agenda

What sets is a result, somehow. A good-bye written
      across the sky with a flamboyant signature –
      or, sometimes, a simple sigh.
Either way, it ends..
Like a life, once lived, can leave in a blaze of glory –
      or just die.
Either way, tomorrow comes – offering yet another
      gift – to be sacrificed...or not

02/22/02

I thought, yesterday, that my goal was to sit on top of a mountain.

I realize, today, that first I need to climb it!

The Art of Completion

Let it stop when it's done
Don't make it run into overtime
    or out of gas
If it's through, let it be.
'Finished' is an awareness that,
    if heeded, allows the recipient
    to place the punctuation

High Noon

My eyes have seen the sadness
My nose has smelled the tears
My mouth's not tasted gladness
Cause my ears heard only fears:

> the moaning of the night
> the wailing of the moon
> the deliberate prevention of light
> except at NOW, High Noon.

This time it can be seen
The veil's temporarily drawn
So – look! I beg you, glean!
What Truth – if allowed – can dawn.

Re-Creation

We wear different clothes and say different things
But, really, it's the same clothes in different colors
           and the same things in different words
Is the Civil War any different from WWII? No...
           the same misunderstanding in different times

Cocoon

My wings are dry
Colors in patterns repeated like Mandelbrot
       will remain clear when I take to the air

They are defined now
Held in place by invisible borders formed only
       by internal purpose.

I entered alone
In the darkness of transition, I learned how
       to emerge together.

Fireflies

Truths flash
too fast to hold in my hand.
'On'…then 'Off'…then 'On'
once more…before gone!

Where? And why?

So close am I to making my
introduction. Do they leave
before it is polite to go?
Or do I?

And where? Why?

Will Power

Some shrews should not be tamed
Some byes are better not lulled
Some thoughts should not be thunk
Some loves are better off culled

Some times are best forgotten
Some tunes should not be sung
Some things are best unfinished
Some bells should not be rung

As life calls from all directions
Inviting us to stray...
To remain upon our chosen path
Requires, often the will to stay

Mirrors and Reflections

A paradox exists between a thing and its mirror
It is impossible to describe because it is the essence of opposites:
Facing the thing, we are opposite it
Facing its mirror, we are the same
We turn
We choose
We are the paradox

Sacred Scars

I kept bubbling over…burning my Self on others opinions, cutting my Self on their sharp haloes. I learned to keep the lid on my joy…to let it ooze into my heart and, there, to dance alone.

Except on certain mornings…when Spring opened me without effort, as if aware that we share the same sunrise. She would send me the scent of honeysuckle and grass being grown.

And on certain evenings when I could hear Yanni's "To Have – To Hold." Then I would begin to glow to the point of eruption, almost. But not quite…

Not because I fear the pain of ignorance anymore. No, I am quite content with the beauty of the wisdom accumulated from the drops of blood shed in the sacrifice of innocence.

The Picnic

I was a martyr! Angry at not being heard, of
being ignored, of having my validity questioned
by The Rules, I retreated into the silence of my
soul – and pouted! As I watched the moon for
signs of safety and whispered to the stars my secrets,
I could feel Night's soothing hands on my brow,
still red hot.

Days would burst upon my serenity like a bugle
calling 'All' to order, forcing It to stand tall, stare
straight ahead and never question The Rules. I
would do Day – their way – knowing that Night
waited in the Western shadows, arms outstretched.

And so I lived – afraid to love.

Until a Day arrived in colors that matched mine.
Galloping over the mountains to greet me, it sang
in harmony to my longing and brought its books
and a blanket. It ordered a river, some wild flowers,
a gentle breeze as an instructor...

And I learned.

Here and Now

We can return to The Garden to be replanted. We can hope for better soil next time – or for more light. But we might not find that spot in the sun…the one by the babbling brook…

So, I suggest blooming where we are – in spite of the apparent hostility toward desire to do so. I suggest fertilizing our existing soil with the Truth that has been gleaned from the lack of good growing conditions…

I suggest using our ability to survive as proof that we can. We can always give up – give in – try again, later. But we are here, now. So why not plant the roots that we harbor within us, heretofore protected by ignorance.

Too wilted from the effort of growing to try? Wilt and wisdom are soul mates. And wisdom is the serpent that pushed us out the door in order to search for it. We are no longer naïve. Why keep pretending that we are?

Duality?

Sculpture begins with 'out'
Form is created by chiseling 'into'
>
> like Time carves into Space to create
>
> like Light cuts into Dark to shadow

Differences only...
Each seen because of the other:
>
> a nose is only visible because of the space
>
> between it and the cheeks

What is a Warrior?

She is tough. But, too, gentle.
She stands firmly upon the internal battlefield
now displaying the blooms fertilized from
experience. The scars in her soul have turned
to stars in her eyes and she can see Heaven.

Yet, she is tolerant of others still waging the
war of Conflict and patient with those insisting
that it wins.

She is Love – but in its new definition: Whole.
Complete. No longer divided by ignorance, she
casts no shadow.

She is a goddess – awakened to the beauty of
One – grateful for the route through Duality for
she knows, now, that to grow wings…one must
fly.

The Prostitute

'She's a prostitute!'
>   we say

>   the tone of our voice judging her right to be one.

Looking away from her,

>   lest we contact the evil we think she is,

>   we live our lives proudly

>   giving our self away

>   in exchange for being accepted

Coma

We get it in Time.
Moments drip into us intravenously
through connections clogged by
forgetfullness

Each drop a particle of Whole, each
complete – but until we open our eyes
all we can feel is the steady tick
of the clock

Independence

A new pattern is emerging - urging its own clarity
so that I may see its face

New colors are forming - storming the door marked
'Yesterday' with determined little fists

New life is throbbing – robbing no other nest in its
quest for freedom

And its egg of Safety is easily cracked - revealing
a golden light, glittering in its own dawn

Vibrating with new energy, yet loving with an ancient
purpose, it weaves its way toward my heart

Recaptured, now, like a dream remembered upon
awakening

Change of Heart

Tell me….
If I dream of a costume
    complete with sequins
        is it possible
            to go to The Ball
                in a simple black dress
                    with a diamond tiara its only adornment?

I mean…
If I wanted it all
    can I settle for less
        when I realize that sequins shine
            only under artificial light
                and can be crushed by a partner
                dancing too close?

Naked

It is impossible to contain Infinity.
You can dress it in different costumes and
arrange its colors in combinations that please,
but you cannot give it a lasting name

To attempt such may appear successful,
for Infinity obeys all desires. But when the
fires finally die and the wardrobes wane into
duplicity causing harmony to become discordant,
infinity will show its true colors by casting aside all
garments

It will stand, in raw power, tamed only by humility,
before wide-eyed innocents and demand nothing –
except acknowledgment

Taste of Life

I've finally lighted
glided to a standstill – and stopped.
Fear of flying kept me fluttering…
Fear of landing kept me standing on time
borrowed from another realm too fast for feet

So wings beat swiftly in indecision.
And heart beat hungrily in desire to taste the
bloom. But fear had locked my gears – and
years fluttered away in a gray haze as I hovered
over open mouths and imagined

Words

I open my mouth to explain 'whole' and find
that what emerges is a 'part'

Thought, in Its purity, understands 'All'
yet when channeled into a word, Its total-ness
is enfolded in its result

Like a child born into a body contains Spirit in
its finest dress, yet must allow it to be worn
one costume at a time, so my words disguise the
very thing they are to illuminate

Yet, if I were silent, would you hear me?

So, I speak – and wonder if the sounds emitted in
apparent control will escape their confinement and
allow their unbridled passion to color their message
into completion

Through the Looking Glass

To go beyond where I am
is to return to where I never left

If I think I left, then I think I must
return

If I know I never left, then I know
I am Home

Nothing changes when I'm back
....except everything

Temperment

Unruffled, now, I am the lake.
Before the sun and moon cast their reflection.
Before the wind divided my waters.
Before time was born.

Unagitated, now, I am my mind.
Before Thought chose corners and donned gloves.
Before thinking stopped dancing in step.
Before fear was born.

I am peaceful, now.
Self-possessed enough to realize it was self who drafted
     my serenity and sent young ideas off to war.

I was a moth - drawn to the flame of Truth - fluttering on
     the threshold of Death - because of desire for more.

Death – a guest we must entertain in order to become the
     butterfly...wings singed the colors of our journey.

Realignment

I am realigning – again.
The shift within is either causing an effect or
      affecting a cause already in motion, allowing
      more colors to surface and make whiter that
      which is still churning with indecision.
Every bit entered is taken in these days – and examined
closely, sometimes harshly, before I remember to finger only
with love the beads of life.

Trinity

I am the eternal essence of Life Itself...the
force created of God, by God and for God...
a piece of The Trinity, a power possible simply
because of its nature.

I am beyond sight and sound yet, too, that
which allows seeing and hearing. I am the
space, even, in between the things seen and the
sounds heard.

Inclusive

My mind shifted
    gears?
    direction?
I don't know. Perhaps 'dimensions'
for I am clear...

Debris once hanging on for dear life
lost its foothold as I turned
    within?
    without?
I don't know. Perhaps both – and simultaneously, too,
for 'here' my sight takes in you

I Am-ness

I have the ability to be you
> and a giraffe

> and a flower growing in another universe

I have what it takes to express as a mountain

> and a river

> and a moon orbiting another planet

Yet I am content, momentarily, being me

> learning of giraffes and how flowers bloom in the Cosmos

> and of rivers and how many moons there are, really

Here, now, I am happy

> discovering you...and mountains

> climbing both

> and watching the sun rise on your faces

Burnished Life

Life tarnishes en route to its goal. It picks
up processes that threaten oxidation and
suffocation by opposition becomes a fitting

epitaph for one birthed in ignorance and afraid
to remove their naiveté. They arrive at the fires
intact, still dressed in purity and step into the

cauldron still trusting in the Lord. And...they
die there. Quickly, but not completely...for
they must return and return again until life becomes

a process of shedding first their swaddling clothes
and then the layers of mis-understandings which
refuse to be polished by friction.

Manifestation

From Uncut
    I cut

From Raw
    I tame

From Whole
    I cleave

From All
    I name

Blowing Smoke

I used to watch, fascinated,
as my Dad blew smoke rings.
Out of his mouth, as he tapped
gently on his cheek,
would billow ephemeral rings,
rotating in a way in which the
smoke created an illusion of a solid ring.

Now I understand:

The universe and everything in it
is created the same way:
rotating subatomic particles
magnetize each other,
creating the illusion of solidity in the
act of motion.
It is the movement, the rotation, that
allows us to see something.
But, in actuality, it is just
…smoke.

Silence

What if I let go?
I won't know my name nor where I live.
What will I give if all that I have is left clinging to
      some vine wearing yesterday's colors?
And if today I am naked…I will have no pocket with which
      to contain my self.

What will happen if I fall?
Or even fly away from the hand that carves
      my life with fingers of such familiarity?

Who will catch my feelings as they flutter from my
      heart like feathers from a dove – free, but
      with no tether to form them into words – what
      will they say?

Savor the Wine

There is a difference between a mystic and an occultist. One is like the chef who takes delicately sliced mushrooms and broccoli flowerets and carrot discs....places them in a Wok, shiny with peanut oil...sautés until just crisp tender, then serves the colorful trio upon a nest of rice, white and fluffy.

The other is the one who sliced the mushrooms, turned the tough stalks of broccoli into manageable morsels and carved the carrots into individual circles...the one who finally found the Wok – hiding in the pantry behind the M& M's...the one who purchased the peanut oil from the International Deli just yesterday.

The chef uses the prepared ingredients with flair and charisma....then invites his guests to dine with a hint of laughter and, perhaps, a glass of wine...

...while the preparer watches from the shadows, corkscrew in hand.

Dear 2011:

I was born looking up; my eyes sought the sky
When a caterpillar crawled, I saw its butterfly
When dark clouds gathered, conspiratorially
I sought the rainbow with childlike glee
The stars always blazed for me overhead
Even when, fear-struck, I convulsed in my bed
"Tomorrow…" I sang and "Tomorrow" again
I never looked back to see where I'd been
Yet strangely, today, I'm aware of the ground
I'm looking down, now, to see what I've found
And, lo, the landscape's not all that bad
In fact, I wonder why it made me so sad
For some reason or other I can't seem to recall
I was like Cinderella – awaiting The Ball
I never noticed how the mice and the birds
Were supporting me, always, with encouraging words
How the sun always rose, no matter the day
And allowed me to bask in its luminous ray
It's time, I think, to blend the two
It's OK to look up – but down's like glue
It keeps my feet planted, firmly, here
So I don't fly away – wondering WHY – next year!

Core Belief

I chose cooperation
     then conflicted with conflict
I chose peace
     then warred with war
To be what I choose
     means BE what I choose
Peace is peace
     all the way to its core!

Entering Now

Do I go into the present from my past or from my future?

Do I give up looking through the ashes of my life relinquishing the need to discover the four-leaf clover that miraculously survived?

Or do I return from some dream I've protected from providence by wrapping it in ego's deception?

Do I rip the brightly colored paper from the box labeled 'Tomorrow' and take it back to 'Now' as a mustard seed?

Or do I boldly take the step toward the door, barely noticeable, within the wall labeled 'Yesterday' knowing my doing so will seal the opening forever?

What awaits me 'Today?'

How will I recognize its face if it is not lined with wisdom or not as yet formed?

For the Sake of Time

Shadows dance here – indiscriminately
Death laughs. Life cries. Judgment is suspended
for the sake of time.

Joy wears black here – and hides its face
in the hands of Night. Fear dresses boldly – its
terror reduced to the hours of a day.

Both play…but hateful games with guns and smiles
with tears and hugs…till no one wins – or loses.
And both die – in a pitiful sigh…

Wondering why.

Sanity

I'm back where I started – again
      wiser for roaming, but then
           when will I learn
                that I need not return
                     cause, always, I'm here where I've been!

Not Yet

Some days
the currents are swift and determined
to empty me like a tree
whose sap turned bitter and hardened into inflexibility
...a summons to the Winds of Change

Some days
the incoming waves upon my shore are no more than shadows
compared to the force that drags my sand away in gluttonous gulps
leaving me exposed to the sun
...never blinking at my plea for mercy

Some days
I almost succumb to the forces of Nature
Attempting to take me with them to some place where I can rest
But not yet...not today.
Today, I have a dream to finish

Arrival

For five decades I sought The Place
though it ne'er seemed to draw near

Every hour - every day
I dreamed of it - year after year

I even tried to take my friends
...all those whom I hold most dear

So imagine upon arrival
my surprise to find they're already here!

The Wild Ride

Be the pendulum…swinging through 'time'
and all its distractions without abandoning the
very vehicle upon which you ride

Do not give into temptation to forget the apex
from which you were born to think you are,
merely, the movement

Or back and forth, to and fro you will go…
becoming but another distraction… and becoming
distracted by other disconnected forms

Holy Ghost

Where do you go when
woe's shadow crosses my mind
and I find the sun no longer shines
in front of me?

Where are you hiding when
fighting erupts from sidelines
unknown and sown seeds sprout
alien flowers?

Where are you – and why
are you not here when year after year
I faithfully light my night with candles
scented with your fragrance?

And why do you leave when I
most need you, depositing but a ghost
in your footprints to guide me through
the grayness of the graveyard?

Understanding

My need to make you understand me
has been replaced by my need to understand
you for, at last, I have learned that
understanding is a circle

The Connection

So many things have come together since I have
So many loose connections found their mark
So many dangling thoughts have ceased to dangle
So many feelings, naked, now aren't so stark
Creative eggs, unhatched, can now be fertile
Paths once very dim can all be lit
Now that I am more connected
More pieces of life's puzzle seem to fit
Yet I am also much more open
Like a bud that's finally learned to bloom
I know this may sound silly
But coming together has…allowed more room!

Fickle

Some days my goals are all in a row
settled like ducks in a shooting gallery
waiting for me to take aim…
Some days they sit quietly
and I tick them off, sure-shot like
their waning numbers a testament to my
ability as a marksman…
Some days, though, my goals take flight
head South for the Winter or
home for the holidays and try as I might to
capture just one, they are last seen
as only gold glints in the sun

Letting Go

Memories burnished from experience
fall from my storage house like
maple leaves when Winter's bugle
causes them to loosen their hold.
Reluctantly, yet bravely, they honor the
final call to duty and in acrobatic dances
with the wind they sway and swirl to their
final resting place…their vivid recall of
detail becoming brittle en route.

Youth

So vulnerable
are the innocent..
A sponge, looking for liquid,
soaking up any it finds, and storing
it in the mind's compartment like
candy - to be removed, later, and
eaten, loudly

What Price Love?

Rather the vine than the fragile flower
Rather the root than the tree
Rather the humble than illusions of power
Rather I AM than me

Yet as the flower releases its essence
The tree gets a whiff of its scent
And —-somehow, somewhere it then knows
How its 'Being' is being spent

Imposter

No use pretending I'm not...
I am!
I admit it
now that I have no choice...
Being not
is not being
and...that is impossible!
I am possible
hidden heretofore
with designer pretense...
Colors so real
one would never suspect...fraud

Dawn

There is a Peace that erupts like a dawn…gently
at first… so soft, in fact, one could return to sleep if
its next step weren't so loud: it explodes its self, a
butterfly emerging from the dark - transition done - its
new wings so colorful they dare one not to notice

There is a Peace whose power alone would render its
definition humorous. A Peace that refuses to be still
and know - one that, instead, needs to demonstrate
Itself - yet how? besides sliding over a shadowed
mountain, causing its dark crevices to see each other
and recognize the vibrant tapestry heretofore hidden
by midnight

Sands of Time

Into the Tempest of Time
we thrust ourselves...again
allowing its hands to mold or to molest our being

Into its hourglass cage
we are born...again
allowing its sands to bury or to expose our nakedness

Time...
to remember its non-existence is to erase
confinement and its confirmation

I wonder:
are there any so courageous?

End of the Line

The Fine Line is not between good and evil
    Such line is a mere delusion
The Fine Line is between All and None
    And, in fact, IT is illusion!

Because no real line exists at all
    How could 'one' be 'two?'
The answer to this apparent question
    ends the paradox 'tween me - and you!

A Real Paradox

It's in the darkest of Midnights
    when you think God is gone
That it's really important
    to LET GO - and HOLD ON!

Refusing Re-runs

How does one recognize Nowhere?
By the joy it ceases to give…
By the death that always threatens
Creator's Plan: to LIVE!

How does one realize No Place?
By the time that isn't real…
By the space that's filled with Nothing
and the way it cannot fulfill.

How does one unlearn such Nonsense?
By seeing Lack as None…
And choosing to go where All Is
…where Never cannot be re-run

Quantum Misunderstanding

I used to be afraid of meeting my self
I thought I'd disappear
So every time I got too close
I'd retreat in a cold, cold fear

Then I realized WHAT would leave
If I got real close to me
And, fearlessly, I wandered IN
To you... and was set free!

Left Behind

Every time I come here
I recognize this place
Its mirror always does its job
by reflecting to me - my face

Yet before I realized "you"
a shadow always came
And covered what I tried to know
before I could learn Its name

Till one night a dream did tell
the truth I'd tried to find
It released the cause of darkness
so shadows were left behind

And in the dawn, next day
the Light arrived re-paired
And when I saw my 'self'
yours as well appeared!

E Equals MC Squared

And then I cried.

A mountain crumbled.

A structure, once a giant, rigid simply in its inability to be anything else, fell...exposing tiny grains of sand.

Thousands - millions! - like pieces of gold. A treasure heretofore hidden behind the structure that they had been...the edifice they had constructed, using their 'selves' as raw material.

What caused their hardness?

When did the tears, unshed, turn to ice until they forgot their original purpose: to flow... and become, instead, a water shed - a form containing content...so busy being the outside that they forgot to look within?

Knowing You

I look at you, now, as I do a sunrise…
never knowing how your eyes will catch the light
until you have unfolded your colors and let them
slide over the mountains in patterns of their own
choosing.

I look at you, now, as I do noon…
never knowing your zenith until your ego cools,
calling shade to temper 'hot' with long, gentle fingers
until streams of twilight spread across your face in
silent surrender.

I look at you, now, as I do night…
never knowing your darkness until you describe it,
never imagining how shadows have had their way with
you unless you choose to show me the scars. Only then,
maybe, will I tell you about the time I thought I knew you.

The End?

Is you me?
Are both we?
Is all they
Or, hey!
Are we all one?

As one dies,
Is I reborn?
If so, as what
Or is it who?

Me? You?

Answer, please
Cause - geese -
I go round and round...
Or is it you
Who do?

A Haiku Postscript

Mystery:

Fragile butterfly
Yesterday a yellow worm
Awesome is your name

Rainbow:

Arch of mystery
Holding treasure chest of gold
In costumed colors

And…..my favorite:

Paradox exists
But so do/does I/me-you
What strange bedfellows!